RAPID HYPNOSIS

Hypnosis on fast Forward

Table of Contents

1.

1.

Introduction

Welcome to the Keys To The Mind training program "Rapid Street Hypnosis."

Street Hypnosis is how many people get their start in the world of personal mastery and was what "Keys to the Mind" originally focused on.

This book was put together to give you the essentials of Street Hypnosis.

It has everything you need to know. With the information in these pages and these pages alone, you could start from scratch and be hypnotizing people within one hour!

Of course, all good things take practice! So, get out there, be willing to fail and to get back up and try again.

The mind is a powerful place, and as a hypnotist, it is your job to

1.

influence minds. You can have a lot of fun with Street Hypnosis, and you're encouraged to get out there and experiment. Just remember that you are in a position of responsibility, and it's essential you take the power you have seriously.

Use hypnosis to empower others, and show them the true potential of the mind.

What Is Hypnosis...?

A friend of mine from New Zealand says there are as many definitions of hypnosis as there are hypnotists.

Some quote the late and great hypnosis pioneer Dave Elman, who said "hypnosis is the bypass of the critical factor, and the establishment of acceptable selective thinking."

Others quote another late and great pioneer, Milton Erickson, who said "hypnosis is a state where the subject shows increased responsiveness to ideas."

Some say hypnosis is a natural state that we all slip into, like daydreaming or reading a good book.

Others say hypnosis is a "special" state

characterized by increased suggestibility.

Personally, I think **hypnosis does not**

exist.

1.

There is no special state in which people are super suggestible. Nor is there an ultimate process which allows you unlimited influence over someone's subconscious mind.

For me,

hypnosis is

simply

"effective

communication.

" Ok, too

boring, too

broad?

Yes, definitely!

Which is why the working definition, we'll use for this book is "**Hypnosis is the influence of the subconscious mind.**"

Often in this book I'll be saying *"hypnosis does not exist!"*

What I mean by this is there is no special 'mystical hypnotic state' – hypnosis is merely a process of influence.

Many of the techniques we'll discuss in this book are based on the old fashioned notion of there being one special 'hypnotic state.'

That is what the **traditional models** of hypnosis are based on.

Induction => special state ('trance') => suggestion => awakening

Personally I think the only phase that *really* exists is suggestion. However, when doing hypnosis for demonstration purposes (which this book will largely focus on) it helps to act *as if* you were working from the traditional model.

Why? The reason is because; this plays into people's beliefs and expectations about hypnosis. Once you do your 'induction' it sends the suggestion that 'hypnosis is happening.'

When people believe that 'hypnosis is happening' they become more open to suggestions because they have a justification for thinking, feeling and behaving differently than they would normally.

In other words *"hypnosis works because people think hypnosis works!"*

Of course, it's not that simple. You will be using a range of powerful psychological devices to influence people's subconscious minds, and ensure that you get the result you want.

The reason why I have explained this to you is so that you can become more

1.

flexible in your thinking.

Yes hypnosis does not exist, and yes, hypnosis is extremely powerful.

If you accept hypnosis as the influence of the subconscious mind, then hypnosis does most definitely exist, and there are thousands upon thousands of effective tools at your disposal to make it happen.

Summary:

Hypnosis "as you see on TV" does not exist. There is no special state. What there is influence of the subconscious mind. When demonstrating hypnosis, it can help to do hypnosis "as if " there was a special hypnotic state. This causes people to believe that hypnosis is happening, which helps them experience things they wouldn't normally permit themselves to experience.

Important: Don't worry too much about theory. I only talk about it here and elsewhere to make sure you don't get trapped in a rigid and old- fashioned way of thinking. Focus on the practical; because this will work regardless of what model or belief set you operate from

The Street Hypnosis Process

Street hypnosis is hypnosis done out in the real world, without the set up and preparation of stage and clinical hypnotists.

It includes hypnosis where you walk up to strangers and do hypnosis with them, as well as when you demonstrate hypnosis with your friends and family.

In this book you'll learn how to rapidly create powerful hypnosis demonstrations on the fly, with *almost* anyone.

So, here's a simple street hypnosis process for you. You need to have the attitude that all these techniques and processes are just *examples*. Use them by all means, but do not be limited by them.

The Street Hypnosis Process:

Intro =>Induction => Suggestion => Awakening Easy, right?

This process allows you to introduce hypnosis to the people you want to work with, or even to a total stranger, lead from the introduction into your induction, flow from there into the suggestion phase, and from there into the awakener.

The suggestion phase is where you demonstrate your hypnotic phenomena, using hypnotic suggestion to demonstrate the power of the unconscious mind, such as sticking someone's hand to the wall, having someone temporarily forgotten their name, causing someone to feel good etc.

When you start doing street hypnosis, you'll find that people are often equally impressed by the induction phase. If you've been floating around the hypnosis world for a while, you may have forgotten just how amazing things that we think everyday seem related to those with no hypnosis background.

Anyway, we will talk more on that later. Now, let's jump into phase 1: the introduction (I'll try and think of a cooler name!)

1.

Introductions and the Pre-Talk Myth

If you've read some other hypnosis literatures, you may have come across the idea that before you hypnotize someone, you need to subject them to a "pre- talk."

The pre-talk is a lecture about what hypnosis is, what it isn't, how it's a safe and natural process, and they won't lose control etc.

Quite frankly, it's a bit boring. When I first started doing hypnosis I'd spent ages on the pre-talk, explaining the science behind hypnosis and everything I thought the person I was working with would want to know. What I learned was, if someone has agreed to be hypnotized they're sold! Feel free to use your pre-talk to build expectations,

1.

and prime their subconscious mind for change and transformation. This is advanced territory, but for simple street hypnosis, you really don't need to bother!

What About Cold Approaches?

People always ask me what to say to someone if you're out and about on the street, doing hypnosis with strangers.

Well, we could spend an entire book just examining this one phase (which is only needed if you're doing 'walk about' street hypnosis, not if you're working with people who have asked you to hypnotize them.)

After a lot of often awkward experimentation, I found that the line that worked best for me was: *"Hey, I'm ..... and I'm a hypnotist. Can I show you something cool?"*

1.

The reason this line seems to work so well is because:

• It *sets the frame* of "hypnosis." This means that it causes people to start thinking that "hypnosis might happen"; and interpret what you do as being the consequence of what "he or she may be doing." Remember in the intro where I described how even though hypnosis doesn't exist, setting up a hypnosis context causes people to allow themselves to think and act in new ways? This early frame setting helps do just that.

• It creates expectation without setting rigid boundaries. You've said "something cool" not "let's do hypnosis." This means that, whilst you have set the hypnosis frame by saying "I'm a hypnotist," you still have the flexibility to do other things. It also gives you a way out if things (I hate this word) "fail" because you haven't tried to do something and *failed*... you've just shown them something cool! (More on failure later).

The Hard Truth:

While a "pre-talk" can be very useful in a therapy / change work context, and is more or less essential for stage hypnosis, for impromptu street hypnosis, it is seldom (if ever) necessary.

Many new hypnotists want to use a long pre-talk just to get them over the fear of failure, and put off the actual induction.

Don't be afraid to dive in the deep end – you'll probably find that's the only way you really learn how to swim!

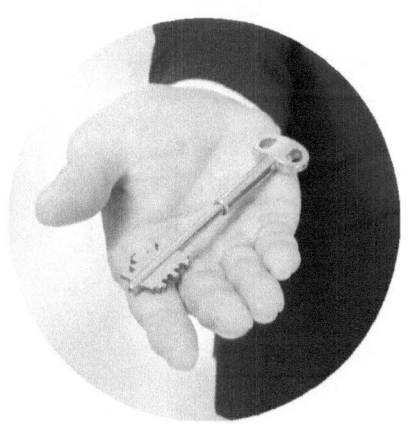

Instant and Rapid Inductions

For many of you, this section will be the only reason why you bought this book! If you've skipped to this section, *stop*, go back, and read the preceding segments. It's important, and you'll learn a lot of stuff that will help you understand this section better!

Ok, ready? Then let's begin.

I said in the intro that hypnosis as we normally think of it does not exist. The role of the instant induction, therefore, is simply to make people *think* hypnosis has happened.

Therefore, the goal of the induction is: *to cause people to believe that they are hypnotized, and act accordingly.*

A better and more practical definition for your purposes would be *"to get people to stop consciously analysing, and respond instead with their imagination."*

Notice how this second definition more or less agrees with traditional models of hypnosis – BUT the emphasis is on the process of accepting suggestions, rather than one ultimate state in which suggestions are guaranteed.

A successful induction does not guarantee your suggestions will be accepted, however, it creates the context that you want.

This isn't about getting people to 'fake it,' it's about engaging in a process which causes people to respond to suggestions. While the idea of a hypnotic state is in my opinion inaccurate, you can create the beliefs, conditions and context which cause people to act as if they were indeed hypnotized.

For practical purposes as far as Street Hypnosis is concerned, it's more or less the same thing.

Don't worry too much about this for now – let's leap into the practical aspect!

For practical purposes, that is what's going on! You are creating a state of mind in which people are more responsive to ideas, even though it's not as rigid or mystical as most people tend to think.

The best instant induction for beginners...

People often ask me what the best instant induction for beginners is.

The truth is... they all are! BUT, when I was new and nervous, I found my best success rate was with what I call "Power Inductions."

Power inductions result when you combine a hypnotic induction with a suggestion phenomenon to create a powerful and self testing rapid induction.

We'll get to those later on in the book. For now, let's begin with your standard instant induction: The shock induction.

The Shock Induction

The shock induction works by creating a small moment of shock or surprise which jolts the conscious barriers temporarily offline. In that brief moment of confusion during which people are trying to figure out what has happened, you can give the suggestion to "Sleep." The "sleep" command slips past their confused conscious filters, and is (in theory) immediately accepted by the unconscious mind. You have just created a brief 'hypnotic trance' – deepened, and you will have hypnosis.

That's the theory I was taught, but experience close to 5 years of experimentation has shown me that, that's probably not really how it works.

What I think actually happens is that the frame you set (i.e. the context you create) causes people to expect hypnosis. You set up the expectations at the start of your induction, and the shock and "sleep" command is just the trigger.

Based on that, I've created a 5 step instant induction process which uses both theories. So it works both for display and in reality. This means you get to do a powerful instant induction which really works, looks powerful and dramatic.

The 5 Step Instant Induction Process

1. Verbally set up trigger

2. Build compliance whilst physically setting up trigger

3. Release the trigger

4. Give the "Sleep" Command

5. Deepen

Let's go over this in more details, and then I'll give you some real world examples that you can start doing right away.

 Important: Before you do ANY of the below, make sure the person you're hypnotizing is securely sitting down, so that they can't fall!

1. Verbally set up trigger.

This is when you tell them exactly what's going to happen, and how they're going to respond. This is actually the most important phase of the entire process!

Let's say you were doing the **Arm Drop Induction**.

 You Can See a Video Demo of This Induction. Just search 'hypnosis arm drop induction' on YouTube.com and there are several of them.

The arm drop induction is when you sit down next to the person you are about to hypnotize, and ask them to push down on your hand. You then move your hand away, and as their hand drops and they experience mild shock and loss of equilibrium; you give your "Sleep" command, and deepen.

Step 1 in the arm drop induction would be to say *"In a moment I'm going to ask you to press down on my hand. Then I'm going to move my hand away; and you're going to*

You are telling them exactly what's going to happen! Remember that though you've told them what's going on, you haven't told them when you're going to pull your hand away. Therefore, they will still experience a moment of shock

2. Build compliance while physically setting up trigger.

This is when you actually get them to do the physical action you're using. In the case of the arm drop induction, it's when you get them to physically move their hand onto yours, palm to palm, and start pressing down.

You can use this phase to build compliance. Compliance is where you get them used to following your instructions, and accepting your authority as the hypnotist. The more they are following your instructions, the less they are consciously thinking. This means they are going to be far more open to the hypnotic suggestions you give.

The way to do this is to be really picky about what they are doing. Do this in a friendly and encouraging way, but make sure you are in control. Ask them to move their position in the seat, use their left hand, rather than their right hand, to push hard or softer, and other similar things.

By the end of phase two they should know what's going to happen. Have them perform a bunch of small tasks on your instruction, and to be expecting and ready for the trigger.

3. Release Trigger

This is when you do what you told them you would do. In the case of the arm drop induction, it's when you move your hand away; and their hand begins to fall towards the ground.

It often helps to wait a couple of seconds before you release the trigger, as this helps to build tension and expectation, and will make the eventual shock factor a lot more powerful.

Remember though that you aim at causing a mild shock— *mild* is the operating word. Confusion is probably a better word than shock; all you are aiming for is a brief point of surprise. So do not jerk arms or yell or do anything that may be harmful or frighten people out of their wits. The true power comes from the expectation you create and the confidence of your delivery; not the shock element.

4. Give Sleep Command

This is the phase where timing is the most important.

Immediately after you have released the trigger, i.e. as the hand is falling, give the sleep command.

Say the word "sleep" firmly and confidently – you do not have to shout it!

Although hypnosis is not sleep, the word "sleep" clearly sends the message that it's time to close eyes and relax. Perhaps, more importantly, it's also what people *expect*. Remember you are using people's expectations about hypnosis to create the hypnotic context, which causes people to respond to your suggestions.

When you say "sleep" most people will at this stage close their eyes and relax into "hypnosis."

Some will not. In fact, occasionally someone might just laugh at you! That's ok – adopt the attitude that **any** reaction is the right reaction! No matter what they do, just say "that's right, now close your eyes..." and go ahead with your deepener.

Anyway, more on failure soon!

5. Deepen

Since there's no such thing as 'trance' there's no such thing as "depth" of trance either. Not really, anyway. Depth is just a useful metaphor for *stabilizing* and *intensifying* the reaction you have been giving.

The "sleep" command will cause people to accept the role of being hypnotized. This is *not* "faking", but, actually believing they are hypnotized and behaving in a consistent manner.

A deepener is a signal for them to continue behaving as they are. Once again, it
stabilizes and *intensifies* the mindset your induction has created.

 **Important:** The number 1 reason why we deepen is so that, after the "sleep" command, people don't open their eyes, look at you, and ask "did that really work?"

The deepener tells them that you are still there and are still in control, that hypnosis is happening exactly how you want it to, and that they are doing fine.

If you are aiming for relaxation, you can use your deepener to help them feel more relaxed. Hypnosis is not relaxation, but relaxation is a useful vehicle to create change, and a state of mind that people associate with hypnosis.

Really *anything* can be a deepener provided it is said with confidence immediately after the sleep command. But to give you some ideas, let's run through a handful of effective deepeners.

Deepener Examples

The Basic 321 Deepener

This is the classic, basic hypnotic deepener, and it also plays right into people's expectations about hypnosis.

After the "sleep" command, simply say *"I'm going to count down from three to one, and with every number I say, you go deeper into hypnosis. 3, going deeper. 2, even deeper; 1, all the way down."*

For basic street hypnosis work, even that is often enough. It's also a great lead in for more 'complex' deepeners like fractionation, which I'll explain very soon.

The Trigger Deepener

This is a nice way to adapt the basic 321 deepener from above. Simple say "each time I (...) you go deeper into hypnosis..." For example, *"Each time I touch your shoulder, you go deeper into hypnosis.*

29

(Touch), Deeper, (touch), Deeper ..."

Fractionation

Fractionation is a powerful way to deepen, and is also very dramatic to watch if you are demonstrating hypnosis publicly.

Fractionation is where you briefly emerge someone from hypnosis, and then re-induct them.

This allows the mind of the person you are hypnotizing to get used to 'being hypnotized', and to respond to your suggestions.

People will naturally become 'more hypnotized' every time you do this. An example of fractionation would go like this:

(You have done the 5 steps of the induction, including the 321 deepener)

"In a moment, I'm going to count from 1 to 3, and when I reach 3, you will return to the room feeling fully awake, and feeling fantastic. The next time I touch you on the shoulder and say the word sleep, you will immediately fall back into hypnosis, going 10 times deeper than the time before..."

This simple paragraph immediately sets up fractionation. It tells them exactly what you're going to do, and how they're going to react. It gives what's called a "post-hypnotic suggestion" to enhance the process.

A post-hypnotic suggestion is a suggestion given during hypnosis which will take effect after the hypnosis is over. In this case, it's the suggestion to go back into hypnosis 10X deeper than the time before.

Because fractionation is a natural effective process, they will naturally go into a 'deeper' state next time. And when they do, it will seem as if your suggestion worked. This acts as a 'convincer' and helps reinforce the effects of what you're doing.

I'd suggest you limit your fractionation to 3 repetitions at most!

 **Important:** When your subject comes 'out' of hypnosis before you re-induct, the hypnotic context still exists which means they are still extremely responsive to your suggestions.

Smile, tell them they're going great, and make them

feel good.

Be careful to act confident, and remind them that they hypnosis is going perfectly, and they are an excellent hypnotic subject.

If you act nervous or insecure, they may feel that they did something wrong, which is not good!

The Breathing Deepener

This is a great deepener to use if you want to create relaxation, especially if you're working with someone who seems anxious or fidgety.

Like fractionation, it's an example of a trigger deepener, with you telling them what they're going to do and experience when something happens. Only this time, they are creating the trigger.

Since deep breathing naturally causes relaxation, and relaxation is something people naturally associate with hypnosis, this can be a very effective and powerful deepener.

Simply tell the person you are working with to take a deep breath, and then let it out slowly and go ten times deeper.

Say that *"with every slow, deep breath you take, you go even deeper into hypnosis."*

If you like, you can make this even more powerful by timing your suggestions to their breathing. Every time they breathe out say "that's right, even deeper..."

Important: There's a powerful hypnotic principle called "**Go There First.**"

What this means is, if you want someone to feel relaxed, your suggestions will be hugely more powerful; you will sound a lot more congruent and authentic if you first feel relaxed yourself.

So, for the breathing deepener, simple take deep breaths yourself, and time your breathing to theirs. You'll notice that this results in a phenomenally powerful deepener than will zone people through the floor!

Instant Hypnosis Examples

We walked through the Hand Drop Induction before, and will get to some more examples when we come to Power

Inductions. However, to give you some ideas, here are some more tried and tested instant induction examples using the 5 step process.

The Arm Pull Induction

Warning: If you're going to do this induction, remember to be **gentle**! Just a super slight tug is required because it's the set up that does the hypnosis, not the 'shock.'

Seriously – it sounds silly (and it is!) but, there have been stories of people actually dislocating peoples shoulders while doing this induction too aggressively! Be gentle – and don't get yourself in trouble!

1. **Verbally set up trigger:**

   "In a moment, I' going to take a hold of your arm. When I pull on your arm and say the word "sleep," you will immediately fall into a deep state of hypnosis."

2. **Build compliance while physically setting up trigger:**

   Take a hold of their arm in one hand, like you're shaking hands, tell them

to swap arms and make eye contact.

3. Release trigger:

Give a GENTLE pull on their arm.

4. Give "Sleep" Command: easy!

5. Deepen

The Hand to Face Induction

(Note: be gentle with this one as well –
no face-palms please!)

1. Verbally set up trigger:

*"In a moment, I' going to take a hold of
your hand and move it slowly towards
your face. When it touches your face,
you will close your eyes, and
immediately fall into a deep state of
hypnosis."*

2. Build compliance whilst physically setting up trigger:

*Take a hold of their hand, lift it gently
so it's above eye level, their palm facing
their face. Tell them to focus on their
palm.*

3. Release trigger:

Move their hand slowly and gently towards their face. When it's about 2 inches away, slowly and gently move it downwards and towards their face so that, when it touches, their face follows and their head is now facing down. Remember: slow and gentle!

4. **Give "Sleep" Command**

as soon as the head touches their face

5. **Deepen**

Take a hold of their hand, and gently move it away into a more comfortable position.

Induction Summary:

1. **Verbally set up trigger**

2. **Build compliance whilst physically setting up trigger**

3. **Release trigger**

4. **Give "Sleep" Command**

5. **Deepen**

The most important steps are Step 1 and Step 5.

It's controversial for me to say this, but the rest is really for show. Don't get too caught up on timing, wording or other technicalities.

Speak with confidence and certainty, and have belief that these will work, and they will.

The Confidence Game

Before we get onto hypnotic suggestions, I need to spend a couple of quick minutes talking about *confidence*.

When I first started reading about instant hypnosis inductions, the books would give a rushed step-by-step approach into shock induction, and then say "hey but this won't work unless you're confident" and leave it at that.

So, let me do you a favour and tell you not

only *why* confidence is essential, but also how to get it.

Why is Confidence Essential?

There are three BIG reasons why it's essential to be confident when doing hypnosis:

- Your subject and the crowd are constantly looking to you, the hypnotist, to see how things are going. If you don't appear to have confidence in yourself and the hypnosis process, then they certainly won't!

  This is particularly essential for instant inductions. Think about step 1, the verbal set up. People are responding to your utter conviction that this will be successful. Your conviction is carried across in the way you act and speak. If this conviction is not there, right from the start, the entire process will be far less effective.

- As the hypnotist, you are putting yourself in a position of authority. In order to speak with authority, it is essential that you seem in control of yourself, and in control of the situation. Giving the game away because of anxiety and unconfident behavior, will only sabotage your work.

- Instant inductions cause a rapid state
  change, and are quite authoritarian
  and direct in nature. Since you are the
  source of the direct instructions, you
  are giving your subject the need to
  come from a place of power. Speaking
  with confidence will give your words
  the impact they need to be effective.

How can you get confidence?

What a question!

First of all, what is confidence? It's a
tricky one. But for practical purposes,
let's call it "belief in your abilities."

That's a very simple definition, so let's
think about it a little deeper.

Think of a situation in which you have
confidence and that, in which you do not
have confidence.

How do you *feel* differently about those
two situations? How do you act
differently? How do you speak
differently? How are your body
language and posture different?

Notice that your speech patterns change

dramatically between when you are confident, and when you are not.

When you are confident, you feel more comfortable in your own skin, and you are more willing to take control.

This is why confidence is essential. So, **here's how to get confidence**:

1. **Practice!**

   When you first start out, you cannot expect everything to immediately go perfect.

   Take a deep breath, and be OK with the fact that:

   (a) you will sometimes feel nervous. And

   (b) not everything you try will always work.

2. Fake it 'till you make it!

Ok, not always the best saying for
life, but, sometimes a very useful one!
Remember the thought exercise from
before? You do naturally know what it
looks and feels like to be confident...
So, fake it! Before you do an
induction, take a deep breath and
pretend that you are feeling super
confident, like you've done this 1000
times before.

It will get easier as you practice, and
eventually— you'll forget that you
even have to pretend!

3. Mental Rehearsal

This helped me big time when I was
starting out!

Go through the hypnosis process in
your head, and mentally practice
every phase. Imagine it going
perfectly, and you are responding to a
range of different reactions with skills
and poise. This will train your mind to
find success no matter what situation
you are given. This will get you used
to doing hypnosis, and thinking like a

hypnotist.

This stuff is important – revisit it when you start doing hypnosis, and you'll notice many of the pieces begin clicking together.

Hypnotic Phenomena, Suggestions and Routines

This is when the "real" magic begins!

Remember, while instant inductions can be very dramatic to observe, the whole point of the induction phase is to get people ready to receive and respond to your hypnotic suggestion.

When doing street hypnosis, every one of your suggestion routines should fulfil three criteria:

1. **To make the person you are hypnotizing feel great!**

2. **To show off the true power and potential of the**

mind.

3. **To keep the crowd (if you are doing a demo) interested and fascinated.**

When working one on one, you have more freedom to go into personal journeys and really focus on making the person you are hypnotizing feel great.

When you're doing a demo, make sure you keep the person you are hypnotizing feeling good, and remember that you do not want the crowd to get bored. So keep it fast and dramatic.

The way to do this is by showing off hypnotic phenomena.

Hypnotic Phenomena

Hypnotic phenomena are everyday mental and physical experiences, which involve the imagination winning out over the rational mind.

There are several basic types of hypnotic phenomena, all of which we experience in everyday life:

Catalepsy.

This is when a part of the body is stuck – technically when the muscles are frozen in equilibrium. In hypnosis this can be a powerful demonstration, for example the hand stick, or the arm lock.

In everyday life, this happens when you ignore a part of your body, and it becomes fixed in place. For example, your arm may become fixed in place when you're having an engaging phone conversation (you don't notice it aching until afterwards). Your legs may be in an uncomfortable position without you noticing when you're engaged in a movie or task, or your neck staying tilted at an odd angle when you're engrossed in conversation.

Ideo-dynamic or ideo-motive movement.

This is unconscious movements, whereby the subconscious mind moves a part of the body without conscious control. In hypnosis, this can be used as part of a powerful demonstration (for example, arm levitation), and for communicating with the unconscious mind; using finger signals (when you ask the mind to twitch a particular finger for yes, and another for no, and ask a series of questions).

In everyday life, this happens when you find yourself nodding along in conversation without thinking about it, twitching as you drift off to sleep, automatically moving to shake someone's hand when they take off theirs. It also involves moving your hands towards your pockets when you worry you've lost your wallet, and moving your eyes naturally when you're daydreaming.

Amnesia

This is when you temporarily lose access to information you normally have readily available. This can make a very powerful hypnosis demonstration! Imagine having someone forget their own name, or forget the number 2, and discover they have 11 fingers!

In everyday life, we call this the "tip of the tongue" phenomenon. It's when you have a word on the tip of your tongue which you are certain you should know; but try as you might to remember it, it stays stuck.

Hallucinations

Hallucinations are often divided up into negative and positive hallucinations. Positive hallucinations are when you see something that isn't there, and negative hallucinations are when you do not see something that is there.

It's often considered the holy grail of hypnosis, to become 'invisible' and use hypnotic suggestions to prevent your hypnotic subject from being able to see you!

Dramatic as this may sound (and is), this

even occurs in everyday life! Have you
ever been searching for your wallet,
looking everywhere, only to find that it
was right in front of you the whole time,
even if you were looking straight through
it? That is hypnotic amnesia!

Pyramiding

If you start right out of the gate and go
straight for hypnotic amnesia with a first
time subject, you may get it, but it's quite
unlikely!

Training people to experience hypnotic
phenomena in a controlled context and
get them 'better' at being hypnotized, as
their conscious mind shuts further down
and they open up to the process, is
laudable. However, it helps to start
"small" and build up.

Begin with comparatively easy to attain
phenomena such as catalepsy, and move
through catalepsy to ideal dynamic
movement, amnesia and then, finally to
hallucinations.

Often in a Street Hypnosis context,
you won't have time to get that far,
which is why I'll be teaching you
ways to use catalepsy, perhaps, the
easiest of the phenomena to get for
great effect!

How to Give Hypnotic Suggestions and Elicit Hypnotic Phenomena

Just like hypnotic inductions,

suggestions too can be broken down step

by step. Here's how it works:

The Six Step Suggestion Process

1. **Describe Desired Result and Give Direct Positive Suggestions For Future**

2. **Use Imagery and Reference Experience**

3. **Repeat 1 and 2**

4. **Issue Challenge / Test Suggestion**

5. **(NOT for Change work) Remove Suggestion**

6. **Test Removal**

As we did for the instant induction, let's run through each step in more detail, using the example of the hand stick.

The hand stick is a hugely popular

street hypnosis routine where you hypnotically stick someone's hand to a wall, desk or a similar object. Seeing someone unable to remove their hand despite straining with all their might is very dramatic. This makes for a fantastic demonstration of the power of the imagination, and of the unconscious mind.

1 Describe Desired Result and Give Direct Positive Suggestion For Future

Like with the instant induction process, this is when you clearly describe exactly what's going to happen; and when it's going to happen.

The general formula for suggestions which involve a challenge, that is the hand stick or name amnesia, is to start with the positive — what they *can* do— followed by the negative, what they *can't* do.

"In a moment, you are going to realize that your hand is stuck to the wall, and you will not be able to un-stick it."

For suggestions like the hand stick, this also has a physical element. It's when you tell them to place their hand on the wall, and tell them that their hand is stuck.

The "For Future" bit means that you are setting up the suggestion for the future, the suggestion hasn't taken effect *yet;* but it will when you say it does.

You can do this in two ways:

a. The post-hypnotic suggestion/trigger method. *"When I tap your hand, you're going to realize that it's stuck to the wall, and you cannot pull it off"* The formula for this is when I... you will. The actual trigger, i.e. the tapping, happens in Step 5, the test.

b. The "not yet, but in a moment" method. This gives you more flexibility, and allows you to test simple by issuing a command. *"Not yet, but in a moment, you're going to realize that your hand is stuck to the desk, and you cannot un-stick it."*

2 Use Imagery and Reference Experience

At this stage they should know
exactly what's expected of them—
be physically ready for it to happen,
and have received a direct
suggestion for what you want to
take effect either "in a moment", or
when you issue your trigger.

It's time to increase the power of
your suggestion.

We do this in two ways, the first
is general imagery, and the
second is a reference experience,
or a real life example.

a) Vivid Imagery and Descriptive Language

This is when your old friend creativity
comes in handy. Using multi- sensory
language (a nasty phrase which really
just means language that covers many
senses, i.e. seeing, hearing, feeling
etc) and descriptive language, tell a
clear and powerful story about what is
going to happen.

This doesn't have to be a novel, just
anything which captures the
imagination and directs them to your
suggestion.

*"It will be as if I have come along with
powerful glue and stuck that hand*

down. That hand is sticking tightly; you can feel it getting stuck to the wall and can imagine seeing the glue binding that hand in place."

b) Real Life Reference Experience

This isn't so important for physical suggestions like the hand stick, but is very important for more advanced suggestions like hallucinations or name amnesia.

The idea of a reference experience is you teaching the unconscious mind how to experience what you want it to.

You are showing them that they do in fact, know how to do what you are asking because; they experience it in everyday life.

I'll talk you through this for name amnesia and negative hallucinations shortly!

3   **Repeat 1 and 2**

What's the one thing that marketers, teachers, hypnotists and daytime TV shows have in common...?

Repetition!

The more you repeat your suggestions,

the more likely it is that they will be accepted, understood and acted upon by the unconscious mind.

After you have given your imagery and / or reference experience, repeat your original direct future suggestion. BUT, increase the urgency too.

So, if the first time you said *"not yet, but in a moment,"* this time say *"In just a moment..."*

Speak a little louder, and a little faster, so that you let the person you are hypnotizing know that the suggestion is about to happen.

4   Issue Challenge / Test Suggestion

Crunch time! This is when you

see if all your hard work has paid

off. This is when you give the

trigger, and / or issue your

challenge.

"Now, attempt to try and un-stick that hand, and notice as it sticks down tighter. Try not, and find it's stuck!"

We'll break down the powerful language used in that challenge in the next section.

When new hypnotists get to this stage, they tend to make a huge mistake.

The mistake is that they issue the challenge, then hold their breath and hope that it will work.

Remember, the key to effective hypnosis is to keep the conscious mind offline by the continual barrage of suggestions and instructions.

This means that after you have issued your challenge, do not give them time to think!

Keep hammering your suggestions, over and over again; *"Try and find you can't, that hand is struck!"*

5   (NOT for Change work) Remove Suggestion

This obviously isn't what you want to do if you're doing change work / therapy,

but for Street Hypnosis and hypnosis demonstrations, it's *extremely* important.

To remove the suggestion, just directly

UN-suggest what it is you suggested, and tell them they are back to normal, and feeling great!

 Important: Even if your suggestion "fails" (more on failure later), still do a full removal and wake up! It makes you look professional, and gives a clear signal that the hypnosis is over and finished.

"That hand is free. You can move your hand normally. Everything is completely back to normal, and you feel great!"

6 Test Removal

In the same way that you tested your suggestion, just test to see if everything's back to normal. Ask them to tell you their name, if you made them forget it. Tell them to count if you made them forget a number, and ask them to move their hand if you stuck it. Simple!

These 6 steps are the basics that will give you exactly what you need to do. Shortly, I'll give you some advanced tips, tricks and techniques you can use to supercharge the power of your inductions and suggestions, in order to make success *almost* inevitable.

More Hypnotic Phenomena Examples

Let's go through the 6- step process with a few more dramatic and powerful hypnotic phenomena examples. Remember the piggy-backing rule that I told you earlier – start with the basic suggestions, and work your way up the ladder of success.

If you're doing multiple suggestions in one hypnosis session, remember to do steps 6 and 7 and make sure the previous suggestion is gone, before you move onto the next one!

Arm Levitation

Arm levitation is a powerful example of idea-dynamic movement, i.e. unconscious movement.

It also works as a great deepener; and is both dramatic and gentle. It's excellent for showing off the true power of the unconscious mind.

Let's go through it step by step:

1. **Describe Desired Result and Give Direct Positive Suggestion For Future**

   "In a moment, you're going to realize that your right hand is floating up in the air, getting higher and higher and higher..."

2. **Use Imagery and Reference Experience**

   "It will be as if 1000 powerful helium balloons are pulling that arm up, getting higher and higher and higher!"

3. **Repeat 1 and 2**

   With a gradual suggestion, like the arm levitation, at this stage you switch tenses, and go from "what will happen" to "what is actually happening now."

"That's right. That arm is being lifted now, getting higher and higher, floating all the way up in the air..."

4. Issue Challenge / Test Suggestion

Remember the magic words: **"Formulas Are Flexible!"** While the test / challenge happens for most suggestions, it doesn't happen for this one.

However, what you can do instead is observe a genuine reaction. If people are faking it, their arm will probably shoot up into the air with noticeably controlled, conscious movement.
If you're observing a genuine unconscious / ideo-motive response, you'll most likely see a gradual, jerky and twitchy moment.

Because this suggestion is particular, repetition is beyond essential – just keep going and going until you get the results; speeding up with each repetition

can suggest that the arm lift is also
speeding up.

5. **(NOT for Change work) Remove Suggestion**

Just tell them that they did great,
and their arm will float down.

6. **Test Removal Pretty easy to spot!**

Hypnotic Amnesia – Name Amnesia

I still remember the first time I succeeded
in getting someone to forget their own
name! It really does hammer home just
how powerful the imagination really is!

Steps 5 and 6 become beyond essential
for this one, make sure you return the
name, and test, test, test!

Like the hand stick, name amnesia
can be very entertaining and even
mind- blowing for onlookers, AND
the person being hypnotized.

Make sure you always treat your subject
with respect, and do not keep it going
too long— just one minute at most will
do!

1. **Describe Desired Result and Give Direct Positive Suggestion For Future**

   "In a moment, you're going to realize that you have forgotten your name, and you will not be able to remember it!"

2. **Use Imagery and Reference Experience**

   This is when you need to use a reference experience. Talk about the 'tip-of- the- tongue' phenomenon, and elicit the feeling of knowing something; but being temporarily unable to access that memory.

   "It would be as if you had it on the tip of your tongue. However, the harder you try, the more you realize it is gone. For the next few minutes only, you will have forgotten your name, and you cannot remember it! That name is gone..."

3. **Repeat 1 and 2**

   You know how this one works! Keep repeating the reference experience until you see that they get it.

4. **Issue Challenge / Test Suggestion**

   "Now, attempt to try and remember

that name. BUT realize that it's gone,
that name is gone!"

Like the hand stick, it's essential that
you keep hammering the suggestion
even after you test! "That name is
gone, you cannot remember it – that
name is gone!"

5. (NOT for Change work) Remove Suggestion

Very important! Give them their
name back! Remind them what their
name is, and tell them that they can
remember it easily; everything is
back to normal.

"Now, your name is back! You can
remember it easily! Your name is
back to (their name) and everything
is back to normal."

6. Test Removal

"You did great and you now
remember your name completely
normally. Tell me your name?"

Hypnotic Hallucinations

Now that you've

worked your way up, it's

time for the big stuff.

Two quick points:

a. Positive and negative hallucinations
    are really the same thing! If they
    positively hallucinate something, they
    need to negatively hallucinate what
    was behind it. Besides, if they
    negatively hallucinate something,
    they need to positively hallucinate
    what was behind it (wow that's a
    confusing sentence!). So, don't get too
    hung up on the difference.

b. While hallucinations seem scary
    and advanced, just like all other
    hypnotic phenomena, we
    experience these naturally
    everyday – remember the example
    of looking for your wallet, only to
    realize that it's right in front of you?

So, because it's so popular in the Street
Hypnosis sphere, let's walk through this
one with the example of becoming
invisible.

This is not something I do often, but I

have done it before, and the reactions are always priceless.

Remember to piggy back- up from other suggestions! Circumstances, in which you feel you have a subject responding well enough and having enough fun to allow you to get this far, won't happen every day – but don't be afraid to seize the opportunity when it comes by!

1. Describe Desired Result and Give Direct Positive Suggestion For Future

"In a moment, you are going to open your eyes and realize that I have become completely invisible – you will not be able to see me."

2. Use Imagery and Reference Experience

"It will be just like when you're looking for your wallet; and even though you know it must be right in front of you, you just cannot see it. For the next few moments only, I have become completely invisible. You can still here my voice, but will not be able to see me."

3. **Repeat 1 and 2**

   Remember to change tense from
   future to present, from *"you will not
   be able to see me"* to *"you cannot see
   me, I am completely invisible."*

4. **Issue Challenge / Test Suggestion**

   Remember to keep the conscious mind
   offline! *"Open your eyes, and find out
   that am completely invisible. That's
   right – gone! You cannot see me."*

5. **(NOT for Change work) Remove Suggestion**

   *"And now I'm back – you can see me
   again. Everything is back to normal,
   and you feel great!"*

6. **Test Removal**

Suggestion and Hypnotic Phenomena Summary:

1. Describe Desired Result and Give Direct Positive Suggestion For Future

2. Use Imagery and Reference Experience

3. Repeat 1 and 2

4. Issue Challenge / Test Suggestion

5. (NOT for Change work) Remove Suggestion

6. Test Removal

Remember to keep it fun when you're doing demos, but make the comfort of the person you are hypnotizing your top priority. Never do anything without their consent, and make sure you treat them with utmost respect.

Warning: Often when you're doing hypnosis with groups, people you are not hypnotizing will start shouting out suggestions.

They'll say "make him do this, and do that..." It is essential that you do not listen to them for two big reasons:

a. Their suggestions will often be embarrassing and demeaning to the person being hypnotized

b. **(Important!)** Even if they make perfectly reasonable suggestions, you must still ignore them. If you accept their directions, suddenly you are not in complete control of the process. As the hypnotist, you must have total control of the entire interaction. So, only listen to do the suggestions that you want to do!

Look at these phenomena as the building blocks. You can take them in any direction you choose. Be creative, and use your imagination.

Alone, they are extremely powerful. If you want to mix them up and make them even more engaging / entertaining, feel free to do so – (provided you keep safety and respect in the forefront of your mind!)

Power Inductions

At this point, you've learned what hypnosis is, and how it works. You've learned how to introduce yourself and get Street Hypnosis started. Besides, you have also learned the 5-step instant induction process and the 6-step suggestion process.

It's time you learned how to combine induction with suggestion to create what I call "power inductions."

These are rapid (yet, not quite instant) hypnotic induction techniques which have three big advantages:

a. They are extremely dramatic to watch – even if they do not succeed!

b. They have a in-built "suggestibility test" so you can see how people are responding before you even begin.

c. They are extremely powerful as first time inductions – if you're feeling

nervous or are working with someone you worry may be 'hard to hypnotize', these power inductions are perfect.

People often ask me what are the best inductions for beginners – I'd definitely say use one of these!

So, let's go over how they work.

I'll go through a big overview in two steps, then break it down piece by piece.

How Power Inductions Work

1. Elicit Hypnotic Phenomena with Direct Open Eye Suggestion

2. Convert Into Formal Hypnotic Induction

Ok, let's break that down a little, and then, I'll give you the step-by-step process.

Step 1: This is when you elicit hypnotic phenomena just like we described in the previous section *without* doing an induction.

Remember, there's no such thing as a hypnotic state! Provided you follow the steps outlined it's easy to achieve basic hypnotic phenomena right off the bat, especially when you remember that all hypnotic phenomena occur naturally in everyday life.

Step 2: This is when you take the phenomena you have, convert and release it into a hypnotic induction. Once you have elicited your waking hypnotic phenomena, their conscious barriers are already way offline. This means they will follow along with virtually any suggestion you give, and will be expecting to play into the hypnotic context we spoke about earlier. In other words, they are already 'hypnotized!' The induction just makes it dramatic, and official.

Let's break this down step by step. Notice that, we're borrowing steps from both the *6-Step Hypnotic Phenomena Process* and the *5-Step Instant Induction Process*.

The 9 Step Power Induction Process.

From The Suggestion Process (Adapted):

1. Physically Set Up and Build Compliance

2. Give direct positive suggestion for present

3. Use Imagery and Reference Experience

4. Repeat 2 and 3

From The Induction Process:

5. Verbally set up trigger and connect to the desired result

6. Release trigger

7. Give "Sleep" Command 8. Deepen

8. Remove suggestion

Let's break this down step by step.

The example I'll use is the "Magnetic

Hands Induction." This is a fantastic power induction, with a massive success rate.

The way it works is that you get them to hold out their hands straight in front of them, shoulder width apart, palm to palm. Have them imagine that their hands are magnetic plates, and are being pulled closer together. Tell them that when their hands touch, they will fall deeply into a state of hypnosis.

Let's break it down.

1. Physically Set Up and Build Compliance

Get them to hold their hands out, palm to palm, shoulder width apart. Carefully position their hands as if you were searching for the perfect position. Be gentle and polite, but be sure you are in control.

2. Give direct positive suggestion for present

The key is for present, unlike the post-induction suggestion process when you are setting up a future suggestion. It is like the Arm-Levitation example. The suggestion begins taking effect immediately.

"Those hands are moving closer and closer together all by themselves."

3. Use Imagery and Reference Experience

"Imagine that your hands are magnetic plates, and that they are being pulled closer and closer together. Those hands are being pulled closer and closer together, magnetically sucked towards each other, moving closer and closer together, pulled by powerful magnets."

4. Repeat 2 and 3

You should begin to see results immediately. Whether you do or not, keep up your suggestion, and keep emphasizing the imagery experience. Increase the intensity, and speak with power and conviction.

5. Verbally set up trigger and connect to the desired result.

This is when you prepare for the induction. In this example, you should begin when the hands are about 3-4 inches apart.

"When those hands touch, you will immediately fall into a deep state of hypnosis. That's right—as soon as those hands touch together, you will close your eyes, allow your head to fall forward, and relax into a deep

6. Release trigger

This is when you get to cheat a little!
Remember your job is to keep the
conscious mind offline? Just before
their hands touch, (when they're about
1 inch apart) gently but firmly push
them together.

7. Give "Sleep" Command

You've now taken control and pushed
the hands together. This is when you
give the "sleep" command,
immediately upon the hands touching.

8. Deepen

Go straight into a deepener – don't
wait!

9. Remove suggestion

This is when you gently guide their
hands in a comfortable position so
that, they are sitting comfortably and
can better experience hypnosis.

Ok, that's a lot of steps, but it's actually
really simple! I've broken it down in so
much detail so that, you know exactly how

it looks and feels in the real world.

I'm only going to give you one more example, but that's ok, because this example is phenomenally powerful.

While the magnetic-hands induction that you just learnt is excellent for first timers, and has a magnificent success rate, this one is probably the most powerful induction I teach for Street Hypnosis.

It's simply called the stiff- arm induction. It's when you get them to hold out their arm straight in front of them, and use suggestion to lock it, so that they cannot bend it.

What makes this induction so powerful is that, you move rapidly from the extreme tension when the hand is stiff to the extreme relaxation when you give your trigger. This creates an extremely powerful experience for the subject, and can create very deep hypnosis.

Because this one is quite physically intensive, it's best to check before you do it that, the person you are working with does not have any arm, back or shoulder issues.

As I say, this induction is super effective, so use it well!

 **Important:** There are a couple of important differences between this power induction and the magnetic hands-power induction. See if you can spot them...

Let's leap right in:

1. Physically Set Up and Build Compliance

Have them hold out one of their arms straight in front of them, shoulder height. Ask them to make a fist, and squeeze that arm tightly.

2. Give direct positive suggestion

Quick question:

What is the difference between the magnetic hands and the stiff arm induction?

The main one is that the magnetic hands induction involves ideo-dynamic movement, whereas the stiff arm involves catalepsy.

Because catalepsy is a phenomenon which requires a test

77

/ challenge – i.e. you are telling them that they cannot do something, it helps to give your direct suggestion for the future, just like we did for most of the hypnotic phenomena examples.

"In a moment, you're going to realize that your arm is stuck in place and you cannot bend it."

3. Use Imagery and Reference Experience

You can make this a lot more powerful and by contrast, hugely increasing the power of the eventual induction.

"That arm is stiff, stiff as a steel bar. Imagine taking all the tension out of your body, and for the next moment only putting it in that arm. That arm is so tense you cannot bend it – move all the tension from the rest of your body into that arm."

4. Repeat 2 and 3

Remember to switch to the present tense – "It is so stiff you cannot bend it."

5. Issue Challenge

The magnetic-hands induction is a gradual continual suggestion. The stiff- arm induction begins with a concrete "success or fail" suggestion – they either can move their arm, or they can't.

To prove to them that the hypnosis has worked; to test the effect of your suggestion, issue the challenge. Remember to keep hammering them with your suggestions, and to do it in such a way that success is inevitable.

6. Verbally set up the trigger, and connect to the desired result

By now their hand should be stuck in place, and they should be trying and failing to move it. If you leave them in that position too long, their harm may begin to ache. So, it's important you move quickly!

This is when you release all the tension you have previously set up, setting up your trigger.

"In a moment, I'm going to take a hold

of this hand. When I do, all the tension will immediately rush out of it; you will instantly close your eyes and relax into a deep state of hypnosis."

7. **Release trigger**

Take a hold of their hand, and as it relaxes, gently shake it to remove the tension.

8. **Give "Sleep" Command**

As you take a hold of their hand, give the sleep command, and immediately follow it up with your deepener.

9. **Deepen**

10. **Remove suggestion**

Make sure their hand is back down in a relaxed and comfortable position.

Power Induction Summary

Like regular hypnotic phenomena this varies, depending on whether you're beginning with gradual phenomena like ideo-dynamic movement, or a success or fail phenomena like the stiff arm.

1. Physically Set Up and Build Compliance

2. Give direct positive suggestion

3. Use Imagery and Reference Experience

4. Repeat 1 and 2

5. Test if doing stiff arm

6. Verbally set up trigger and connect to desired result

7. Release trigger

8. Give "Sleep" Command

9. Deepen

10. Remove suggestion

Get out there and use these! You'll be
surprised to discover just how powerful
and effective they are!

Safety and Awakeners

You now know how to do hypnosis! You know how to hypnotize people with instant and rapid inductions, and lead them from there into powerful suggestions and hypnotic phenomena. You also know how to do power inductions which are fantastic for both first- time hypnotists and first- time hypnotic subjects. It will surely give you an amazing success rate.

BUT, before you even *think* about doing hypnosis, it's essential that you learn how to wake people up!

 **Important:** Indeed, hypnosis is NOT sleep, and YES there is no such thing as "hypnosis" in terms of a hypnotic state. Despite this, it's still essential you always do a good, clear and complete awakener after every hypnosis demo.

Here's why:

a. By doing "hypnosis", you are creating the hypnotic context and leading people through an experience they label as hypnosis. To send a clear signal to all people involved, especially the person being hypnotized, it's essential you do a formal awakener to say that the hypnosis is now over, and everything is back to normal.

b. Even though "hypnosis" doesn't exist, you have definitely been influencing people's subconscious minds, and changing their beliefs. This is powerful, and it's important you make them believe everything is normal. The mind responds to beliefs, and when people believe everything is back to normal, it will be.

c. Although hypnosis is not relaxation, by doing hypnosis you often create deep relaxation. As a clear signal that now is the time to start and feel alert, always finish on a clear awakener.

Remember: Although "hypnosis" as you see on TV and in the movies does not exist, the reactions you are creating are real, and for the purposes of Street Hypnosis, you might as well act *as if* hypnosis exists!

How to Do an Awakener

An awakener should always accomplish three things:

a. Return people to a normal state of energy and alertness

b. Street Hypnosis (not therapy) completely removes all hypnotic suggestions, and emphasize that everything is back to normal

c. Leave them feeling happy, relaxed and positive

Provided you clearly accomplish all those three things, you can say whatever you want.

Just do not rush your awakener! Take time on this, as it's one of the most important phases in the entire hypnotic process.

Here's a sample script which accomplishes all these three points, using imagery and counting to help emphasize the suggestions and get the reaction you want.

Note: I *hate* "scriptnosis" – that is teaching hypnosis simply as scripts for people to read. However, the only phase where I think it's OK for you to use a prepared script is the awakener... provided you make it your own! Change the words around, and make it yours, but know it by heart, and do not skimp on this process!

"In a moment, I'm going to count from 1 to 3. When I reach three, you will be fully awake, alert and aware. Everything will be completely back to normal, and you will feel fantastic. 1. Coming up now. 2. Everything back to normal and you feel fantastic. 3 All the way back now, open your eyes and discover you feel great!"

Remember to keep increasing your energy as you go through it! Speak with passion and emphasis. Remember, **go there first** and bring yourself into a high energy state of alertness, to help you lead them there.

Key Tip: The Post Hypnotic "Trance"

Remember that after people come out of hypnosis, they are still extremely suggestible.

I've seen countless new hypnotists blow it by doing a perfect induction and wake up, only to look nervous and say "um... did that work?" upon the wake up.

As soon as they open their eyes, smile confidently and congratulate them. Tell them they did great, and that they feel fantastic.

Don't Run Away!

After you've done your awakener, hang around for a few minutes and chat. Just be there to make sure they feel fantastic, and answer any questions they have about hypnosis.

Keep emphasizing that hypnosis is a safe and natural process, which allows them to tap into the positive power of their subconscious mind.

The Abreaction

Again – hypnosis is a safe and natural process. However, you are influencing people's beliefs, which put you in a very powerful position. Take this responsibility seriously.

While this book DOES contain everything I think you need to know to get out there and start doing hypnosis, you'll benefit greatly if you get yourself to a live training, and get some practice and supervision.

An abreaction is when, during the

hypnotic process, people access unpleasant memories which they may have previously locked away, and freak out.

This should not happen during street hypnosis – it's really only relevant for therapists. Just to be on the safe side, let me run through how to avoid and deal with them.

How to Avoid an Abreaction

The big one is, DO NOT do any regression work – ever! Do not go anywhere near childhood memories or anything vaguely linked to any form of regression, unless you have specialist training. This is a biggie!

The next is to make sure you keep the entire process positive. Although, a full scale abreaction is phenomenally unlikely, during basic phenomena like hand stick and name amnesia, people can occasionally become scared.

This is why it's essential you constantly frame everything in the positive. Make a habit of what I call "the feel good rule".

The Feel Good Rule:

With every suggestion and phenomenon you give (from the hand stick to name amnesia, arm levitation and hallucinations), add in the phrase "and this will feel great because it shows you just how powerful your mind really is."

With that one sentence you stop people from being scared, and make the entire hypnosis experience a positive comment on the power of their own mind.

It is essential that you avoid anything uncomfortable, embarrassing or risky. Do not try anything beyond your skill level; and keep everything positive and cheerful.

If people begin feeling uncomfortable, calmly and confidently end the hypnosis. Be sure to undo the suggestion and run a full wake up.

How To Deal with Abreactions.

This is from an article I wrote about how to deal with abreactions.

Again, this is a Street Hypnosis book! The chances of you experiencing an abreaction are so remote that I almost feel silly talking about it... HOWEVER, better to be safe than sorry, right?

1. **Stay Calm**

   You are the hypnotist. You are in control. No matter what is going on in your own head; you need to breath deep, be calm and exude confidence.

   Handle this like a professional, confidently and congruently. As Douglas Adam says, 'Don't Panic!' Stay calm, and sort it out smoothly.

   If you are struggling to be heard

over the clamour of the panicking
subject, then stay calm and use
repetition, an authoritative yet
reassuring tone.

2. Avoid Physical Contact

Not only could physical contact
seriously freak out the person
experiencing an abreaction, it could
also create an anchor to the negative
state. Obviously, you want to avoid
this as the last thing you want is that,
all the emotional baggage they are
dumping on you to be released again
the next time some- one holds their
wrist, or places a hand on their
shoulder.

3. The Magic 9 Words

Gerald Kein is the source of these 9
words which have now become very
famous among hypnotists.

They work well, and will more often
than not, be all you need. Say them
calmly and confidently:

"The scene fades and you tend to your

breathing.' Simple!

These 9 words should bring them from the trouble state they are in, and pull them back into reality. However, that is not always enough.

How To Make Sure It Is Done Right

The possible trouble with the above is that, it doesn't really go after the cause of the abreaction.

Now we do not want to start doing therapy here (unless you are properly trained and in an appropriate context) but, we do want to firmly shut the lid on the memories causing the abreaction and safely ensure that they go back to where they were beforehand.

How do we do this?

We talk directly to the unconscious mind.

We give process instructions that explain exactly what it needs to do, in order to ensure the well being of the hypnotic subject.

We explain to the unconscious mind that a memory has been revealed to the conscious mind before the conscious mind is ready, and explain to the unconscious mind that it must continue to protect them from this memory until the conscious mind is ready to deal with it on its own (otherwise this may create dependence of therapists etc).

Use language like 'protected' and 'stored', rather than 'locked' or 'imprisoned' when describing the revived memory, otherwise you may worsen the problem.

Here's an example:

"I am now going to talk directly to your unconscious mind.

In the past, you have been doing a good job keeping (name) safe from these memories.

It is important that you continue doing this. Store these memories away back in the safe place until such time that, the conscious mind is ready to deal with them on (his / her) own.

Keep the conscious mind safe and protected, and remove from it from all memory of this incident. Leave to the conscious mind only what it is capable of processing on its own right now; hide the rest until such time as it is fully ready.

So, now as you sit there, the memories are stored back away, and the scene fades. You tend to your breathing, and emerge only at the rate and speed that everything can be restored to its ideal, healthy balance. Everything is well, and you return feeling fine"

The memory is returned to the safe place where it was before, and amnesia is created for the abreaction itself so the subject does not have the added trauma of that experience. They are returned to a healthy state of affairs with the unconscious mind looking after them properly.

Often doing this can stop an abreaction before it starts, and prevent the memories from being fully uncovered, before the abreaction really begins. Make sure you have your wits about you and are always keeping a very close eye on the people you hypnotize. So, if something does begin to happen you can nip it in the bud.

Be sure your subject is

totally 'fixed' before

you emerge them. There

are no absolutes.

The one thing I am

absolutely sure about is that

nothing is absolute. As you

develop more confidence,

always trust your

unconscious.

Rely on what comes to you in the moment. Use these words and techniques as guidelines only.

How to Avoid Physical Harm

Ok, so now you know how to do a solid awakener, avoid and deal with abreactions. You also know the "Feel good rule" to keep all suggestions positive, and to ensure people constantly feel positive and comfortable.

You also know the importance of returning everything to normal, and making sure you undo all suggestions you give.

The final key is just to avoid causing physical harm. This is pretty simple, and I'd like to say it's all common sense, but I'll spell it out just to be sure.

a. Control the crowd! Make sure they don't interfere with the hypnotized person, and keep them at a safe distance

b. Do hypnosis away from roads, traffic
    and obstacles! People often lose
    spatial awareness while being
    hypnotized – stay clear of cars!

c. Have them securely sitting! It may
    look cool to do a standing, instant
    induction and drop someone to
    the floor. However, it's just not
    worth the risk.

d. Be gentle! No hard tugs please. Soft,
    gentle. Allow the expectations and
    the set up to do the work.

Legal Stuff

Before you start doing hypnosis, I
strongly suggest that you check out
your local laws. See if you need any
licensing or certifications, and if they
have any restrictions on what you can,
and cannot do. It's always better to be
safe than sorry.

PHEW! Ok – Back to the fun stuff!

Take safety seriously – this stuff matters!
Read over these guides again, and commit
a solid awakener to memory. When
you've done that, let's leap into the deep
end and discuss some advanced street

hypnosis tricks of the trade...

Advanced Patterns for Certain Success

At this stage in the book, you already know the basics! You know what hypnosis is, and you know how to do it quickly and safely.

Believe it or not, even if this book was the first thing you have ever read on hypnosis, you are now head and shoulders above most of the hypnosis world!

Street hypnosis is the cutting edge and, sorry to mix metaphors, you're riding the crest of the wave!

What I want to do now is to give you a bunch of devices and language patterns that will help you increase the success of what you're doing.

To give you a food metaphor, you have the meat and potatoes, now it's time for the spices and the sauces.

This stuff really helps, but the

fundamentals are even more important! 1000 fancy language patterns are often no match for one, confidently given direct suggestion.

This stuff helps, and it can make a huge difference, but don't get too distracted by the glitz. Remember the basics are where it' really at.

When you're learning, I'd recommend doing hypnosis purely with the basics you have already learned.

Then, I'd come back to this list, and focus on one pattern or device at a time. By practicing only one at a time, you stop yourself from getting confused and keep the basics in mind.

After only a handful of inductions, you'll be integrating these techniques naturally into what you do, and creating powerful results without even having to think about it.

Advanced Street Hypnosis Patterns...

The Bind

The bind is when you tie to ideas together, "the more you (...) the more you (...)"

In street hypnosis, it's particularly powerful for challenge phenomena, like the hand stick or name amnesia.

"The more you try to remember that name, the more you find it's stuck."

By linking the two ideas together, the very act of trying to un-stick their hand causes it to become more stuck – trapping them into doing what you want.

Try and Find

The word "try" implies failure. If I said to you "try and pick up that glass of water", you'd suspect that I did something funny with it.

Notice in the examples I gave, the challenge always took the form of *"attempt to try, and find you can't."*

"Attempt to try" is like saying "try to try" – it is two layers away from success, and heavily implies failure.

The "and find you can't" immediately tells them exactly what you want, and gives a clear, simple positive instruction which they can do "find you can't."

Dissociative Language

When you're getting someone to give up conscious control over something, it helps to separate it from them. So, if you want someone to be unable to move their hand, call it "that hand" rather than "your hand." If you want them to forget their name, call it "that name."

When you end the suggestion and undo it, use associative language again, as in "you can now move *your* hand."

Presupposition of Awareness

A presupposition is a statement which can only be understood and processed if certain facts are assumed to be true.

A presupposition of awareness shifts the emphasis from "will it work" to "are you aware that it is working?" – implying that it has already worked.

This is why we say *"In a moment, you will realize that your hand is stuck to the wall."*

Use words like realize, notice, discover and (from the earlier example) find to shift people into an awareness presupposition. It's a powerful stuff!

Presupposition of time

Like the awareness presupposition, a presupposition of time shifts emphasis from whether to when. It implies that what you suggest is going to happen – the question is only when it does.

Let's look at the Magnetic- Hands Power Induction.

"When those hands touch, you will fall into a deep state of hypnosis."

The presupposition "when they touch" obviously implies that they will, but here's how to make it even more powerful:

"Do not go into a trance until those hands touch."

This is very powerful. It implies that those hands will touch and that they will go into a trance, and puts you in complete control over the entire process. It's a very nifty wee sentence!

Let's combine a couple for the hand-stick example:

"Only when you're sure that that hand is completely stuck, attempt to try and un-stick it, and notice that it sticks tighter..."

"Only when you're sure" is an awareness presupposition. It's also a powerful trap which ensures that it's their responsibility to fully stick their hand before they attempt to pull it off – more or less making your success inevitable.

These quick techniques will really help you achieve success and get results. Practice one at a time, and soon you'll be combining mastery of the fundamentals with linguistic wizardry, that will virtually guarantee your success.

How to Preventand Deal WithFailure

The worst nightmare of the new hypnotist is to do an instant induction or attempt a hypnotic suggestion, only to find out that it fails.

Before I give you some techniques, tools and strategies for dealing with and preventing failure (so smoothly that, it will look like everything was planned) you need to get one thing:

Failure is your friend!

Tattoo this on your forehead! (Not literally – but you get the point, it's very important!)

Let's go through the worst case scenario (I know it well – I've been there!)

You start learning hypnosis; you get out there and start telling all your friends about it.

They go "ok, hypnotize me, hypnotize
me!" and eventually, nervously, you say
"yes". You stumble through an induction,
say all the words right, and your friend
just laughs at you, eyes wide open.

Um... SO WHAT!

Failure is part of learning the game. You *need* to be

cool with it.

If you spent your life waiting to be 100% certain that
failure will not happen, you
will never get anything done – ever!

Accept failure as part of the learning game
– make it your friend! Ok, do you get it?

Only when you really get this is time to
move on.

Strategies For Preventing and Dealing With Failure

The number 1 attitude you need have beyond "failure is your friend", is one of utilization.

Where new hypnotists go wrong is, if something deviates just minutely from their mental plan, they panic.

You need to adopt an attitude of mental flexibility.

Adopt the attitude that every reaction they give you is the correct reaction.

No matter what they do, be smooth and unfazed. 9/10 (especially with practice) you'll find a way to convert it towards success, but even if you don't, if you look smooth and confident you'll save face regardless.

To illustrate how utilization works, let me tell you the story of my very first instant hypnosis induction.

My first ever instant hypnosis induction:

A bunch of friends gathered round to watch me try the magnetic- hands power induction which I've just taught you.

I did it *terribly* and even though her hands moved together, when they touched and I said "sleep" she just started laughing.

I said *"that's right – now keep laughing, and find you can't stop laughing. Now close your eyes, and find that the more you laugh, the harder those eyes stick together. Those eyes are stuck together, and you cannot un-stick them!"*

It worked! She was laughing as she struggled to open her eyes! After the hypnosis she said it was one of the most amazing things she'd ever experienced – and I was the only one in the crowd who thought anything had gone even slightly wrong!

Utilization requires you to think on your feet, but here's an overview of the process:

1. **Keep cool!**

2. **Encourage the behaviour "that's right... keep..."**

3. **Tell them to close their eyes**

4. **Deepen**

Simple! You have taken their behaviour, used it, and continued unfazed. Masterful!

When doing hypnotic phenomena, the same process is true - remember the attitude that every response is the correct response.

Be creative with this.

If you're doing a hand stick, but they manage to lift their hand, convert the lifting hand into arm levitation.

If they remember their name when you said they wouldn't, tell them to remember just how powerful their memory is, and to remember a time when they drifted off into a deep state of relaxation – lead from there into an induction!

The possibilities are endless! Flexibility and creativity are your two greatest tools
– remember that every response is the perfect response!

Occasionally, you will find someone who you just can't hypnotize. That's cool – don't sweat it! Tell them that "maybe you just weren't in the right mood today" and stay positive and polite.

Remember to run a full wake up even if you only get partial hypnosis, just to be on the safe side!

Taking It To The Next Level with Rocket Launch Tactics

You now know how to do Street Hypnosis! You know how to approach people "hey, I'm a hypnotist, can I show you something cool?" Do an instant induction; elicit powerful and dramatic hypnotic phenomena. Then, combine phenomena and inductions to create a power induction. You know why and how to act confidently; and also how to avoid and deal with failure. You know the safety essentials of Street Hypnosis, and how to prevent and deal with abreactions.

Before I send you out into the street, I want to give you one final tool that will dramatically supercharge the power of what you do.

A mentor of mine taught me this powerful way of turning a normal and impressive hypnotic phenomena demo into something truly life-changing.

Here's how it works:

When you create hypnotic phenomena,

people are suddenly in awe, and their conscious barriers are offline. Even simple phenomena like the arm levitation or the hand stick are extremely powerful, and get a massive emotional reaction too.

It's a shame to leave such a powerful emotional state to waste. So, why not attach to it a powerful, positive and motivational suggestion.

The hypnotic phenomenon is the rocket; and the suggestion you attach to it is tied to the rocket—it takes off with it.

Here's how to do it:

1. Create hypnotic phenomena

2. Attach hypnotic phenomena to suggestion

3. Release phenomena to complete metaphor

Number 3 is optional, but it really can tie everything together and create something very potent.

Let's go through it with an example.

1. Create hypnotic phenomena

You've learned the hand stick – so let's do this one. Imagine now that their hand is stuck to the wall.

2. **Attach hypnotic phenomena to suggestion**

"In the same way that that hand is stuck to the wall, at some points in your life, you may have found yourself stuck down to a problem that you did not know how to get out of."

The positive suggestion is now set up for the trigger, and linked to the hypnotic phenomena.

3. **Release phenomena to complete metaphor**

"But in the same way that that hand now easily comes free (tell them their hand is free!), so too can you easily free yourself from problems, and discover you had so many more resources available!"

See how powerful this process can be?

Let's run through the basic 2 step process with arm levitation:

1. **Create hypnotic phenomena**

Their arm is now lifting up into the
air

2. Attach hypnotic phenomena to suggestion

*"In the same way that arm is now
lifting higher and higher into the air
all on its own, so too can you realize
that you have powerful resources
available to you — that you can use to
get what you want from your life, and
unleash your true power and
potential."*

It doesn't have to be too fancy –
get into the habit of adding a
positive suggestion that makes
people feel good to every
phenomenon you use.

If you are in doubt, just use the "feel-
good formula" from before *"and you feel
great because you realize the full power
and potential of your own mind."*

 **Important:** Hypnosis is what
you make it. It can be a cheap
parlour trick... or it can be
something which inspires
people, and leaves them
reeling with the possibilities
and potential you have
opened up for them.
Recognize the power of the
unconscious mind, and do it

You Have Just Spotted The Tip of the Iceberg...

You now have all the tools you need to get out there, and do street hypnosis. However, this is just the beginning!

Street Hypnosis was the start of the journey for me, and it has taken me to places I could never have imagined.

It's not just about "hypnosis" – it's about mastering the mind.

Learn how to get the most out of your mind, and help others do the same.

Whether you want to increase your own confidence and improve your inner game, become more persuasive and influential, start a lucrative new career or increase your success in the business and marketing world, understand how to work with your own mind, and speak to others in such a way that gets right through to who they really are— the possibilities are unlimited.

Wishing you the greatest of success with this information, and the rest of your journey towards mastering the mind!